# GLOBAL QUESTIONS

# How Should We Tackle Crime?

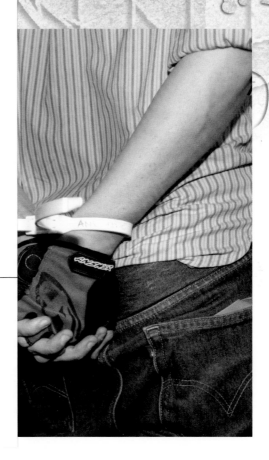

**Anne Rooney**

W
FRANKLIN WATTS

First published in 2010 by Franklin Watts

© 2010 Arcturus Publishing Limited

Franklin Watts
338 Euston Road
London NW1 3BH

Franklin Watts Australia
Level 17/207 Kent Street, Sydney, NSW 2000

Produced by Arcturus Publishing Limited,
26/27 Bickels Yard, 151–153 Bermondsey Street, London SE1 3HA

Series concept: Alex Woolf
Editor and picture researcher: Jonathan Hilton
Designer: Ian Winton

Picture credits:
Corbis: title page (Richard Cohen), 6 (Jose Fuste Raga), 7 (Bettmann), 8 (Lee Snider/Photo Images), 9 (Mercury Press/Sygma), 10 (Andy Rain), 11 (China Photos/Reuters), 12 (Gianni Dagli Orti), 13 (Bettmann), 14 (Carl & Ann Purcell), 17 (Thierry Orban/Sygma), 18 (Ashley Cooper), 19 (STR/Reuters), 21 (Vincent Kessler/Reuters), 22 (Shaul Schwarz), 24 (David de la Paz/epa), 25 (Harish Tyagi/epa), 27 (Ralf-Finn Hestoft), 28 (Ted Soqui), 29 (Yves Sygma), 30 (Scott Houston), 31 (Luis Galdamez/Reuters), 32 (George Esiri/Reuters), 33 (Reuters), 35 (Shaun Best/Reuters), 37 (Amy Toensing/Sygma), 38 (James Leynse), 40 (Bazuki Muhammad/Reuters), 41 (Reuters), 42 (Reuters), 43 (Wairimu Gitahi/Reuters).
Science Photo Library: cover (Jim Varney).
Shutterstock: 36 (interphoto).

Cover caption: Carefully masked and gloved to avoid contaminating potential evidence, a police forensics officer examines the firing mechanism of a revolver.
Title page caption: The police remain our first line of protection against criminal activity.

A CIP catalogue record for this book is available from the British Library.

Dewey Decimal Classification Number: 364

ISBN 978 1 4451 0064 7

Printed in Singapore

Franklin Watts is a division of Hachette Children's Books, an Hachette UK company.
www.hachette.co.uk

SL001354EN

# Contents

# Chapter 1

# What is crime?

Every society sets limits on the behaviour it will tolerate. These limits are recorded in the form of laws, and breaking these laws is regarded as a crime. Crimes in modern societies range from relatively minor acts, such as parking a car in an area where parking is not allowed, to extremely serious acts, such as murder, rape and terrorism.

All crimes are antisocial acts in one way or another, and all societies need to protect themselves and their citizens against criminal activity. In general, behaviour that offends society in some way is punished – the more serious the crime, the more serious that punishment tends to be.

## What counts as a crime?

Different things are important to people at different times and in different places. Although some deeds are crimes everywhere, such as murder, other acts are not as clear cut. An act that is a crime in one society may be perfectly acceptable in another. This is because laws reflect social values and sometimes also religious beliefs. For example, in Western countries it is legal for adults to drink alcohol, but in some Muslim countries it is illegal; in Ireland it is illegal for a woman to have an abortion unless her life is at risk from the pregnancy, while in other European countries abortion on demand is legal.

## Assessing crime

People commit crimes for a wide variety of reasons. Most societies distinguish between acts committed on purpose

**The Supreme Court is the highest judicial body in the USA. A case heard in a lower court may be referred to the Supreme Court if the verdict is challenged.**

**Patty Hearst was kidnapped by the paramilitary Symbionese Liberation Army (SLA) and, she claimed, brainwashed. She joined in the SLA's criminal activities, including this bank robbery. She was jailed for her crimes, but later pardoned as she was held not responsible for her actions.**

and those carried out by accident, between those that are premeditated (planned in advance) and those carried out on the spur of the moment. Many also take account of whether the perpetrator was wholly responsible for his or her actions.

## Rising crime rates?

Many people worry that crime rates are rising and that society is becoming more dangerous. There has always been crime and older people always claim that criminal activity among younger people is worse now than it was in their time. It is difficult to tell whether there really is more crime or if more crimes are simply being reported. People have become more willing to report some crimes, such as rape and domestic violence, because the judicial system has come to take these crimes more seriously and to be more sympathetic to the victims. Fear of crime rarely matches the true likelihood of being the victim of a particular type of crime. At present, many people are afraid of terrorism, yet each individual is at very little risk.

## Expert View

**Protecting victims**

Many victims of distressing crimes are reluctant to carry through the process of reporting the crime and attending court because it is too upsetting. In Australia, children and the victims of sexual assaults no longer have to sit in court, but can attend by video link.

'Victims of crime, particularly those who have experienced sexual assault, have suffered enough and require all the support that can be given to help them through the trial process.'

*John Hatzistergos, Attorney General, New South Wales, Australia, 2010*

## Acting together or alone

Many crimes are committed by individuals acting alone. Muggings, burglary, dangerous driving, tax evasion and drug taking are common examples of this. Other crimes are committed by gangs – either small local or neighbourhood gangs or large international groups. Terrorist organizations may be national or international in composition. Some crimes are even committed by nation states against other states or social groups.

## Organized crime

Organized criminal gangs operate like full-scale businesses. They are highly structured organizations that build their criminal empires by keeping people in fear. Around the world, groups including the Mafia (an Italian-American organization from Sicily), Chinese Triads, Japanese Yakuza and the Russian Mafia have been able to control businesses, the police and even national governments.

## Terrorism

Terrorism is the use of violent acts and threats to create terror and to intimidate people in order to achieve a political or ideological goal. Terrorist acts often target innocent civilians who have no connection with the cause or conflict. The increase in terrorism over the last 20 years has led to greater fear and, as a result, more laws that aim to protect people from terrorist acts.

## State crime

Even governments who set the laws can be guilty of committing crime. In some countries governments have been accused of torturing political

**The best known act of terrorism of recent years was the destruction of the World Trade Center in New York City in 2001 by the Islamic organization al-Qaeda. Several countries have introduced new anti-terrorist legislation in the aftermath of this attack and other terrorist acts.**

**When children kill**

In 1993 two ten-year-old boys murdered James Bulger, then aged just two years, in Merseyside, England. The murder was similar to scenes in a film called *Child's Play*, which features an evil doll that tortures and kills people. The two boys had watched the film the night before and the judge who sentenced the boys believed that it had influenced their behaviour, though officers investigating the crime disagreed. The press ran the story for weeks and some even called for a ban on violent videos.

**CCTV (closed-circuit television) footage shows the toddler James Bulger being led away by one of his young killers.**

opponents or of political corruption, such as accepting bribes. This type of crime is more difficult to detect because the three main groups involved – politicians, police and government regulators – are in a position to cover up evidence of their wrongdoing far more effectively than ordinary people.

## How we think about crime

The media is often accused of sensationalizing crime – of making it seem exciting or glamorous. There are many films, books and TV series in which crime and the fight against crime are a source of entertainment, and crime is frequently covered in news and current affairs programmes. Many people suspect that there is a link between watching violence on screen or playing violent computer games and violent behaviour in the real world. Although most people who view on-screen violence will not act it out, a small minority may be more easily influenced by what they watch. Links between crime rates and the representation of crime are difficult to prove, but crime in entertainment is certainly a factor in how we think about and imagine crime. The reality of crime is often very different from the way it is represented by the media and entertainment industries.

## Treatment of suspects

People accused of committing crimes are called suspects. In the case of serious crimes, suspects may be held in prison until their trial. If the crime is less serious, they may be released on bail – allowed to go free as long as they comply with certain conditions, such as providing an amount of money or agreeing to stay within a certain area. Before the trial, the prosecution (working on behalf of the state) and the defence (working on behalf of the suspect) prepare their arguments by gathering evidence and statements.

## Court trials

At the trial the prosecution and the defence each present their case. The trial is a formal debate between the two sides, managed by a judge and often observed by a jury. The judge aims to make sure that the arguments are presented fairly and in line with the law, and that everything is clear to the jury. When all the evidence and arguments have been presented, the jury retires to discuss its verdict – the decision

**Suspects often try to keep their identities hidden from the media. Being thought of as a criminal can have a serious impact on an individual's life, and even if that person is later found to be innocent, the damage can be difficult to undo.**

These young boys accused of being pickpockets in China face a harsh penalty if found guilty. Some people do not report crimes if they disapprove of the penalty that may be imposed. If this happens, then laws do not work properly to protect society.

about whether or not the accused is guilty. The jury presents its verdict and, if the accused has been found guilty, the judge passes sentence based on laws that set out the penalties for different crimes.

## Setting the sentence

Judges can often vary the sentence according to the circumstances of the crime. For example, someone who shoots and kills a stranger in the street is likely to be convicted of murder, as is a person who kills a brutal partner after 20 years of violence and abuse. The different circumstances, however, may lead a judge to impose a harsher penalty on the first offender. The law cannot be administered fairly by following the rules alone. Human input, compassion and consideration of all circumstances are essential.

## FOCUS

**Too long ago?**
In December 2009, John Demjanjuk went on trial in Munich, Germany, for his part in the Holocaust, which took place more than 50 years before. He was so old and ill that he had to attend on a stretcher. Doubts were raised about whether there is a point beyond which it is pointless to put a suspect on trial. One such doubt was discussed by Matthew Norman, political commentator on *The Independent* newspaper.

'The greater questions than that of his guilt, however, are perhaps whether justice of any kind is served by trying him now . . . and if so, whether the desire for justice or for vengeance is the paramount motive for the trial.'

# Chapter 2

# How did we deal with crime in the past?

As soon as people began to live together in structured societies they needed laws to set limits on what was acceptable behaviour in order to protect individuals and society as a whole. When people broke any of those laws they were punished. If it was not clear whether or not an individual had committed a crime, that person could be questioned, or sometimes tortured, and then punished if found to be guilty.

Early societies did not have a police force, lawyers or a network of prisons and probation officers to manage convicted criminals. Punishment was usually swift and brutal and often involved mutilation, execution or banishment. Even so, some civilizations developed the start of a judicial system we would recognize today. The ancient Egyptians, for example, had a type of police force that served the pharaoh. Members of this force wore a golden *Ma'at* pendant – Ma'at was the goddess of truth, order and justice. When criminals were caught they were taken before trained Egyptian officials in a court who decided the appropriate punishment according to laws laid down by the pharaoh. There were many laws, and punishments included being branded, exiled, drowned, beheaded or burned alive.

## Legal codes

The earliest known legal code is that of a Babylonian king, Hammurabi (1792–1750 BCE). His system of laws lists 282 crimes and their punishments, and was originally recorded on 12 carved stone tablets.

**Hammurabi's stele (a stone slab or column), which contains the code of laws of the Babylonian ruler.**

An engraving of a scene in ancient Rome depicting the emperor Trajan, considered as being one of the more enlightened rulers, giving an audience in his court.

One of the meanings of the word 'Draconian' we use today refers to laws that seem very harsh. Draco was a Greek lawgiver and in his legal code, written in about 622 or 621 BCE, nearly all crimes were punishable by death, even extremely minor ones.

## An eye for an eye

Legal codes often try to match the severity of the punishment with the seriousness of the crime. The Torah, for example, sets out the ancient Hebrew legal code, where it states that a person who costs someone a hand or an eye shall lose his or her own hand or eye in turn. This 'tit-for-tat' principle has been used throughout history. It is harsh, but it sets a limit on retribution.

## Torture

Most modern judicial systems try to discover whether or not someone accused of a crime actually committed it before imposing any sort of a penalty.

## FOCUS

### Preparing for torture

John Gerard was a spy, accused in 1597 of being part of a plot to overthrow Queen Elizabeth I of England:

'We went to the torture room in a kind of procession, the attendants walking ahead with lighted candles.

'The chamber was underground and dark, particularly near the entrance. It was a vast place and every device and instrument of human torture was there. They pointed out some of them to me and said I would try them all. Then he asked me again whether I would confess.

'"I cannot," I said.'

*John Gerard, who was tortured before escaping from the Tower of London*

In the past there were less rigorous methods of cross-examining witnesses in court and no advanced forensic techniques. Instead, many societies used torture to try to extract the truth from the accused.

Torture involves deliberately causing physical or mental suffering in the hope and expectation that the person will reveal what they know. Of course, most of us would say anything at all just to stop the torture and so provide unreliable information or lie. Torture is still used in some countries, even though it is against international law.

Tests of physical endurance were also used in medieval Europe as a method of trial. The idea was that God would show if people were innocent by enabling them to survive an ordeal or win an unequal fight.

## Thinking about justice

In eighteenth-century Europe, ideas about what it meant to be human, and the role of the individual in society, changed. Instead of simply punishing someone for doing wrong, new thinkers began to ask whether criminals could be helped to reform and become useful members of society –

**The stocks were used in Europe and later in America as a way of exposing offenders to ridicule, shame and abuse by passers-by. The stocks shown here are real, but are now a historic attraction on St George's Island, Bermuda, where tourists can take their turn in the frame.**

whether they could be rehabilitated. This new way of thinking progressed through the nineteenth and twentieth centuries, and the harsh punishments of the past were eventually phased out. In today's world, most developed countries concentrate on crime prevention and the rehabilitation of offenders.

## Justice in the New World

In the seventeenth century, many Europeans made the sea crossing to America to the New World. All brought with them beliefs in God and the law. The English system of common law combined with Spanish and French ideas of civil law. The legal system they established had lower courts to hear petty crimes and higher courts to rule on more serious offences.

By the nineteenth century a police force had been set up and penitentiaries (prisons) were built in various states to 'confine wrongdoers and correct their criminal behaviour'. Similar moves were under way in parts of Europe at the same time.

## Uneven progress

While the United States, Australia and many European countries made progress during the twentieth century towards the more humane treatment of criminals, this was not the case everywhere. In the former USSR, for example, millions of people died in gulags – harsh prison camps. Prisoners were forced to carry out hard labour in freezing conditions, and were given very little food. Abuse by prison guards was common. Even within the United States, the hard labour of the chain gang remained as a punishment in some states until 1955. Groups of prisoners were chained together and forced to do hard, physical work, such as building roads and breaking rocks.

# FORUM

**Few people would consider the more horrendous punishments of the past to be acceptable now. But are physical punishments ever justified?**

'No one shall be subjected to torture or to inhuman or degrading treatment or punishment.'

*European Convention on Human Rights*

'I believe that the removal of corporal punishment was a mistake, and the consequences are still being acutely felt with another generation of smart alec kids creating all sorts of havoc.'

*Adrian Watson, member of Antrim District Policing Partnership, Ireland*

## What's your opinion?

# Chapter 3

# How do we deal with crime today?

Today, developed countries generally have well-established and fair judicial systems. Each country has its own set of laws, set down in its statutes. There is a police force to investigate crime and to work to prevent crime. There is also a system of trials so that people accused of crimes have every chance to defend themselves, and there are penalties for those found guilty, ranging from fines to imprisonment or, in some countries, execution. Even though there are differences in the details of judicial systems in various countries, the principles are much the same. The aims are to protect society, to maintain justice and to punish and rehabilitate prisoners, while ensuring that the accused receives a fair trial and is protected from injustice.

## Making laws

Most countries' laws build up over time. As society changes, some laws become out of date; they may stay in force, but are not used. There is still a law in Sweden, for example, setting out the punishment for releasing too many pigs into an acorn wood, yet few Swedes today keep pigs. New laws are created to meet new needs. Rules about online crime were not needed before the Internet. The rise of international terrorism has led many countries to pass new laws to try to prevent attacks.

When new laws are required, the government usually consults not only legal experts, but also experts in the areas that will be affected by any

## Expert View

**In an attempt to prevent terrorist acts, a British law allows suspects to be kept in prison without trial:**

'Detention without trial is an erosion of the rule of law that should never have been contemplated . . . even in terrorism, there have to be trials based on evidence . . .

'The only acceptable alternative to trials is to put suspects under surveillance and to . . . [make] sure that they are aware that their every movement is monitored.'

*Helena Kennedy, human rights lawyer, 2004*

**Sometimes there can be conflict between religious and civil laws. These French Muslims are protesting against the civil law that prevents them wearing a hijab (headscarf), which their religious laws say they must wear.**

changes. For a law relating to Internet piracy, for example, politicians will take advice from computer experts and the entertainment industries. In countries with democratic governments, the laws often reflect the general wishes and concerns of the population. In countries where the government is not elected, the people have less say, or even none at all.

In some countries laws are based in religious beliefs and are often rooted in a religious text. Legal systems based on ancient texts sometimes struggle to take account of new developments, such as mobile phones, guns and the Internet. In such circumstances, religious experts are called on to discuss how the law must be interpreted.

## Law enforcement

Many countries have police forces to keep law and order. The police work to prevent crime, to encourage people to report offences, to investigate crimes that are reported and sometimes to prosecute criminals. The police force is usually funded by the state, and in some countries it is linked to the army. In countries that have a judicial system based on religious laws, religious leaders may play a part in law enforcement.

Some crimes are carried out by a small group or by individuals – burglary, rape or murder, for example. These are generally reported by the public. Some crimes, however, are very complex, such as fraud, tax evasion or drug running. To discover these, specialist police teams, sometimes working undercover, search for evidence of criminal behaviour. Police forces of several nations may even work together to tackle international crime.

## Reporting crime

Police can investigate a crime only if they know about it. You might think that someone who has been harmed by a crime will report it, but that is not always the case. Sometimes people fear the distress of being involved in a court case, especially if the crime was itself very distressing, such as a physical attack or rape. Sometimes they think there is no point in reporting the crime because the police will not find the culprits – if their bag was stolen on a train, for example, or their pocket was picked. And sometimes embarrassment or the fear of revealing their own criminal activity stops people reporting a crime. Some large businesses, for example, do not prosecute employees who have embezzled money or cheated on their expenses because they fear the resulting publicity will be bad for business.

**Crime-scene investigators comb an area of land looking for the tiniest clues that may help them solve a crime. Vital evidence may range from clothing and tyre tracks to tiny traces of hair, fibres or pollen.**

## Investigating crime

Forensics – the science of investigating crime – involves many techniques. Some of these are familiar from television crimes series – fingerprinting, detailed examination of physical evidence and the scientific investigation of blood traces. Experts will look at such clues as the type of pollen on the clothes of a body, which might show where the person was killed, or analyze handwriting evidence. In countries where the police are well funded and efficient, much information can be gained from forensic investigations.

The police also rely on tip-offs – members of the public, and sometimes other criminals, passing on information about a crime that is planned or about someone who has been involved in a crime. Information from the public must be treated carefully to

# FOCUS

### A victim of mugging

'They just started punching me in the face, downward swings, really hard into my face. I fell to the ground.

'They kicked me in the face. They kicked me in the head. I was just saying like "get away from me, get away from me", just screaming. So scared, thinking that the next step after this . . . I'm going to be killed.'

***Mugging victim, Port Costa, California, USA***

avoid people deliberately trying to get someone into trouble who is not actually involved in the criminal act. Occasionally, allegations of crimes are made maliciously – with the intention of harming the accused – even though no crime has been committed at all.

## Preventing crime

It is always better to prevent a crime in the first place than to solve it after it has happened. Police and governments spend a lot of time and money on crime-prevention measures.

Methods of preventing crime include improving security, educating people to avoid crime, maintaining a visible police presence to deter crime and installing CCTV to monitor high-risk areas. If people know that their activities are being watched, they are less likely to break the law. In some countries, crime prevention requires a more active and aggressive role on the part of the police, with armed officers keeping the peace in difficult situations. In times of unrest or rioting, police are sometimes given additional powers, though this in itself may feed unrest if people then fear that the police will be unfair or aggressive.

**Armed police in a shanty town in South Africa struggle to keep civil order. After years of apartheid and its associated injustice, there are many poor black people in South Africa. Conflict between different groups, and between rich (mostly white) citizens and poor (mostly black) citizens, is common.**

## Guilty or not guilty?

In many economically developed countries, people accused of a crime are given the opportunity to argue their defence in a court of law. They can challenge the evidence presented by the prosecution, trying to prove that they did not commit the crime, or they may give reasons for committing the crime that could affect the court's decision. If the accused cannot afford legal representation, a lawyer may be appointed by the court to help defend that person. These measures are intended to make sure people have a fair trial. Some cases are decided by a jury. A jury is a group of ordinary people, often chosen at random, who decide whether the accused is guilty or not on the basis of the evidence and arguments presented in the court. The judge then decides what should happen to the offender if found guilty and passes the appropriate sentence.

## Not always fair

Fairness is not a characteristic of all legal systems around the world. In China, for example, people are often arrested, given a show trial and rapidly punished without having a proper chance to defend themselves. Similarly quick and unjust methods are common in many countries suffering political unrest or unelected governments. During the military dictatorship in Argentina (1976–83), many political enemies of the rulers were imprisoned without trial, tortured and executed. These were political prisoners: their crime was opposing the ruling party. Injustice like this is common in many parts of the world.

## International crime

Sometimes the international community takes a stand against crimes against humanity and the unjust treatment of prisoners. The International Court of Justice in the Hague tries to settle disputes

### Expert View

**Tackling crime depends on effective law enforcement and people taking personal responsibility:**

'Yes, we need more cops on the street. Yes, we need fewer guns in the hands of people who shouldn't have them. Yes, we need more money for our schools. Yes, we need more jobs and more job training and more opportunity in our communities.

'But we also need families to raise our children. We need fathers to realize that responsibility doesn't end at conception. We need them to realize that what makes you a man isn't the ability to have a child – it's the courage to raise one.'

*Barack Obama, 9 September 2008*

between states and gives advice to states considering international activity (such as military action). The court is part of the United Nations. It may rule on disputes about borders and resources, for example. The European Court of Human Rights and the Inter-American Court of Human Rights both work to protect human rights and to prevent and try crimes that violate human rights in Europe and in North and South America.

**People disagree about the aims of penalties for crime:** I'm not interested in what will be good for the criminal – I don't care. He killed my son and I just want revenge.

We must leave personal feelings out of justice. If a person can be rehabilitated and become a useful member of society, that is more valuable than just punishing him.

***How do you think punishment and rehabilitation should be balanced?***

**A Kurdish demonstrator protests outside the European Court of Human Rights in 2004 against the imprisonment of Ocalan, the leader of the PKK terrorist group, which has carried out assaults inside Turkey to further its case for an independent Kurdish state.**

# Chapter 4

# What are the causes of crime?

It is easy to think that people who commit crimes are simply bad or selfish, but it is not always as clear cut as that. People can be driven to crime by many factors, including anger, greed, desperation and strong beliefs. There are many social factors that contribute to crime, but there are also individual motives.

## Poverty and crime

Poverty is an important cause of crime. When people do not have enough money to live on, they may be driven to crime by despair. In areas where there is a great difference between the rich and the poor, some poor people may have to follow a life of crime in order to survive.

A child, led by desperation, steals a piece of meat in the aftermath of the major earthquake that destroyed Haiti's capital city, Port-au-Prince, in February 2010.

Even where people have enough to live on, or have social support from the state, they may still turn to crime if they are envious of those around them who have better, more affluent lives, or if they consider it unfair or unjust that they are poor.

People who are socially disadvantaged are more likely to become criminals. Factors that increase the likelihood of a young person growing up to commit crimes include a lack of education, poverty, poor housing, a broken home life, neglect or abuse, drink or drugs used in the home, mental illness and unemployment. It is estimated that 40 per cent of the prison population in the United States are functionally illiterate, which means that they are not able to read or write well enough to cope with the normal demands of society. Crime may seem the only way out for these people.

> # FOCUS
>
> ### Crime waiting to happen
> According to research in the UK carried out for the Joseph Rowntree Foundation in 2002 by the Communities that Care (CtC) organization, nearly 25% of older youths aged 15 and 16 and 10% of 11–12-year-old boys had carried a knife or other weapon during the past year. Almost 20% of 15–16 year olds and 8% of 11–12 year olds admitted attacking someone with the intention of hurting them seriously.

## Drink and drugs

Many crimes are committed by people either under the influence of drink or drugs, or desperate for money to buy them. Drug misuse is itself a crime, but it is connected to many other types of criminal activity, including drug production, drug dealing, smuggling, money laundering, prostitution, street violence and gang warfare.

## Violence breeds violence

People who have experienced violence themselves, perhaps in the home or in a violent neighbourhood, are more likely to be violent in turn. Fear may lead people – particularly young men – to carry weapons, such as guns or knives. If they are armed, they are more likely to commit a violent crime, but they are also more likely to become the victim of violence. This creates a vicious circle in which people carry weapons because they are afraid of violence, and because they are carrying weapons they are then more likely to become a victim of violence, thus increasing fear levels still further. Gun crime is much more common in the USA, where people are allowed to own and carry guns, than in the UK, where it is difficult to acquire a gun and illegal for most people to carry one.

These members of violent youth gangs, known as Maras, in Honduras, have tattoos, body piercings, aggressive-looking clothing and weapons – all part of their gang 'uniform' and identity.

## Fighting society

Not all criminals act alone. Some are members of gangs or even organized crime rings. The motives for joining a gang may be fear, the desire for a better life, greed or simply a generalized anger at society.

Anger at perceived social injustices is behind many crimes of vandalism and some personal assaults. People who feel that society has let them down or has not equipped them to find a good job and have a fulfilling life sometimes destroy property and lash out at more fortunate people around them.

Other reasons why young men join gangs and commit crimes are to boost their self-image, to make themselves look tough and to draw admiration from others. Wanting to look good in front of their peers or girlfriends can lead to dangerous criminal activity, such as joyriding, drink-driving and acts of aggression.

## Criminal responsibility

Usually for people's actions to be considered criminal they must be held responsible for what they have done. With children and people with mental disabilities, it can be difficult to decide whether they really knew what they were doing or the consequences of their actions. The age at

| Country | Age of criminal responsibility |
|---|---|
| USA | 6 (in some states) |
| Ireland | 7 |
| Scotland | 8 |
| England & Wales | 10 |
| USA | 10 (federal crimes) |
| Canada | 12 |
| Netherlands | 12 |
| France | 13 |
| Germany | 14 |
| Italy | 14 |
| Japan | 14 |
| Russia | 14 |
| Denmark | 15 |
| Finland | 15 |
| Norway | 15 |
| Sweden | 15 |
| Portugal | 16 |
| Spain | 16 |
| Belgium | 18 |
| Brazil | 18 |
| Peru | 18 |

which people are held responsible for their acts is called the age of criminal responsibility. This varies between countries (see chart, left). The decision regarding responsibility may hinge on whether the child or mentally ill person is thought able to know right from wrong, or whether he or she can distinguish between levels of seriousness in acts that are wrong.

## Corporate crime

Crimes committed by businesses, or corporations, are usually the result of greed, ignorance or neglect. In 1989, the oil tanker *Exxon Valdez* ran aground and spilled more than 40 million litres of crude oil into the waters of Alaska's Prince William Sound, causing a major ecological disaster. The captain of the tanker, who was drunk at the time of the accident, was sentenced to 1,000 hours of community service. The company, Exxon, which was responsible for the tanker and its captain, had to pay approximately $5 billion (about £3 billion) in damages. Corporate crime may also be committed against individuals or groups of people. In 2010, the US Department of Agriculture had to pay $600 million (about £360 million) to Native Americans for failing to treat them equally with white Americans when giving loans and grants for farming programmes.

## FOCUS

### Cutting corners costs lives

A serious example of corporate crime occurred in 1984 when a chemical plant in Bhopal, India, owned by a company called Union Carbide started leaking poisonous gas. Inadequate safety checks were held to be responsible for the tragedy. As a result, about 3,000 people died in the days immediately following the leak. But some estimates put the ultimate death toll much higher – perhaps as many as 20,000 people.

**Demonstrations finally led to some measure of compensation for victims of Bhopal, even though it took 20 years. No one has been prosecuted for the disaster.**

## Accidental crime

Occasionally, people are ignorant of the law and do not realize that they are committing a crime. Sometimes they may commit an offence by accident or through negligence – perhaps because they didn't predict the outcome of their actions. Someone who drives while drunk may be found guilty of unlawful killing after an accident, even though there was never any intention to harm anyone. If crimes are committed by people accidentally then there will be no motive, but a court still has to decide whether they were acting unreasonably and whether they should bear responsibility for what they did.

## Crimes of passion

People who, under normal circumstances, are law abiding may in a moment of anger, anguish or other strong emotion lash out. People who plead that their actions were a crime of passion do so to show that their acts were not premeditated: they acted on the spur of the moment. They may plead diminished responsibility or even temporary insanity, and in some countries this may be taken into account when sentencing them.

## Revenge and honour

Although a crime of passion must be committed in the heat of the moment, there are many instances of revenge attacks and honour killings that are premeditated. In some communities, male family members believe it is their right and duty to take physical

## FORUM

**Does someone's bad life experiences ever excuse criminal behaviour?**

• Some people think that individuals will usually turn to crime only if their experience of life has led them to it, but others feel that we are all responsible for the choices we make.

• If someone is denied opportunities to make a good life for themselves, they cannot be blamed if they use crime to challenge injustice – society is to blame.

• Everyone can strive to get a better life by legal means. Not all poor or disadvantaged people turn to crime, so background is no excuse for criminal activity.

*What's your opinion?*

The family of American doctor David Gunn mourn at his funeral after he was murdered by an anti-abortionist on his way into his clinic in Florida. Strong belief in the rights of the unborn child in the USA have led to terrorist threats and attacks on people who work in abortion clinics.

revenge against daughters, wives or sisters who have sex with someone other than their husbands or who refuse to marry the husbands that have been chosen for them.

## Belief

Some crime is carried out not for material gain or to harm an individual, but to make a point, bring publicity to a cause or promote a belief. Direct action – taking a non-democratic route to try to bring about social or political change – often involves criminal activity. It ranges from peace protesters storming army bases to non-payment of taxes. The organization Plane Stupid in the UK protests on environmental grounds against the expansion of airports. Its activities have led to some protesters being arrested.

## Terrorism and politics

The twentieth and twenty-first centuries have seen a rise in terrorism. Terrorists are motivated by a strong belief in a cause and are willing to kill others and often themselves to further their aims. Some terrorists are motivated by religious fervour and some by a political agenda. The Tamil Tigers, a terrorist group in Sri Lanka, employ extreme action in their struggle to win a self-governing Tamil homeland in part of Sri Lanka. Al-Qaeda is a terrorist group that fights against non-Muslim beliefs, practices and influences, particularly in Muslim states. Vandalism, violence and even murder have been perpetrated by people opposed to abortion or animal experiments. Terrorists cannot usually be deterred by threats of penalties and are sometimes attracted by the prospect of death and martyrdom.

# Chapter 5

# Which penalties work?

Most modern countries have a range of penalties for crimes ranging from fines to prison sentences. In some places, the death penalty is used, but usually only for very serious crimes. Under sharia law, which is used in some Middle Eastern countries and elsewhere, penalties include physical punishments such as flogging.

## Lesser punishments

For less-serious crimes a fine is sometimes considered to be a sufficient punishment. There are other non-custodial sentences (those that do not involve going to prison), including electronic tagging, orders covering behaviour (such as staying away from someone or some place) and community service orders (which require offenders to work in the community to help other people). An electronic tag shows the offender's location at all times, so a probation officer can tell if that person is in a place he or she is not supposed to be, or is outside after an agreed curfew time. All these punishments are cheaper for society and less damaging for the offender than imprisonment.

## Rates of imprisonment

Worldwide there are more than 9 million people in some form of prison, including people on remand (waiting for a trial). In 1999–2003, England and Wales had 142 people in jail per 100,000 head of population, while the average in Western Europe

**A seriously overcrowded prison cell in California, USA. Conditions like this are extremely stressful for prisoners and staff alike. Violent outbursts are common when prisoners are kept in poor conditions.**

A cell in a modern prison in France. The prisoner has privacy, personal washing facilities and a television. Instead of just punishment, the prison system in France aims to rehabilitate prisoners and equip them for a useful life after their release.

was just more than 100. In the United States, 715 per 100,000 population are in prison, with one state (Louisiana) having 1,013. In Canada the figure drops to 116 and in Australia it is 114. Japan is lower still, with 54 people per 100,000.

## Why we use prisons

Modern prisons have several aims. They protect society from dangerous criminals by keeping them locked away, they punish people by taking their freedom from them, but they also aim to rehabilitate prisoners – to equip them through education or counselling to live without reoffending after they are released. How well prisons work to deter crime, protect society and rehabilitate prisoners depends on how they are organized and run. In South-East Asian countries, such as Thailand, prisons are overcrowded, often infested with vermin and there are few or no opportunities for prisoners to exercise or take part in meaningful activity. In modern European prisons, the emphasis on rehabilitation is greater and conditions are generally much better.

## Expert View

'During 2002, concern about prison overcrowding led Britain's senior judge, Lord Woolf, to discourage judges and magistrates from sending criminals to jail.' At this time, the prison population was rising and the crime rate falling. 'The implication is that judges and magistrates are deploying a rather barbaric instrument when everyone else in Europe prefers a more gentle approach.'

*CIVITAS – Institute for the Study of Civil Society*

A prisoner in Estrella Jail, Phoenix, USA, shows the cuts on her wrists that are the result of a failed suicide attempt made while she was in prison. Inmates may stay locked in their cells for 23 hours a day unless given a work assignment.

## Problems in prisons

There are many problems in prisons that can limit their effectiveness. These include drug misuse, violence and overcrowding. It is estimated that half of all prisoners in Western Europe are addicted to illegal drugs, and nearly 70 per cent of prisoners aged between 16 and 29 had used illegal drugs in the year before they were imprisoned.

In addition, many people sent to prison have mental health problems and there is a much increased risk of suicide within the prison population. Between 2002 and 2003 there were 105 suicides in UK prisons. Many prisoners report suffering from depression for many years before going to prison.

Violence in prison is almost routine. Many prisoners are regularly abused, bullied, threatened or assaulted and are too scared to report the abuse or violence. Some prisons have confidential helplines for staff, prisoners and their families to report violence. The extent of violence in prisons varies dramatically around the world.

## Is prison a deterrent?

Keeping people in prison is an extremely expensive option for the state. Providing prison facilities and staffing them are costly, and the state also often has to make welfare payments to prisoners' dependants if their jail terms leave their families without an income. If sending people to prison cut crime and led to successful rehabilitation, it would be worth the cost. But the evidence suggests that prison does not work well and

A bloody prison riot in El Salvador has left some prisoners injured and others dead. Prison riots are most common when conditions are poor and the prison system underfunded.

reoffending is common after release. In the UK, the reoffending rate within two years of release is running at nearly 60 per cent. Many people worry that prisons have become 'schools of crime', where young, first-time offenders are locked up with hardened criminals who teach them additional criminal skills.

Long prison terms don't seem to reduce crime rates. Colombia imposes the longest prison sentences of any country in the world, yet has most kidnappings and very high rates of murder, assaults, shootings and stabbings.

## Focus

'If large numbers of extremely antisocial human beings are penned together in disgusting conditions, they will become more antisocial, not less. If opportunities for education and rehabilitation are few . . . the possibilities for reform will be correspondingly reduced and the bad men who are sent to prison will come out worse, not better . . . It may seem curious that [these prisoners] could have any redeeming features at all, but their will to survive is, in its own way, a tribute to the human spirit. That they can only do so by becoming as bad as the conditions in which they are kept is inevitable.'

*Radmila May,* **Contemporary Review,** *1999*

## Sharia law

Sharia law is a code based on Islamic religious teachings that covers conduct in all areas of life. It lists a set of crimes, called Hadd offences, as well as the penalties for breaking them. Penalties can include flogging, death by stoning and having a hand cut off. It is simply not possible to tell whether or not these severe penalties work as a deterrent, since many of the countries involved have inadequate systems for recording crime, especially crimes that are committed in their more rural areas.

**Nigerian Hajara Ibrahim, 18, weeps with relief after winning her appeal against the death penalty from an Islamic appeal court in 2004. Although pregnant, she had been sentenced to death by stoning by a sharia court for having had sex outside marriage.**

## Capital punishment

Capital punishment, or judicial execution, means taking someone's life as a punishment for crimes committed. The death penalty is still used in 58 countries around the world, including the United States, China, India and Indonesia. These are countries with large populations; around 60 per cent of the world's population lives in countries that execute people.

The death penalty exists in federal law in the United States and is used in some, though by no means all, states. In the state of Texas, 447 people have been put to death since 1976. China has the highest execution rate in the world, and in 2008 it put to death 5,000 prisoners. The death penalty is not used anywhere in the European Union.

**Protesters on the streets campaigning against the death penalty in the USA. In 2008, 37 out of the 50 American states allowed executions. The first state to abolish the death penalty was Michigan in 1847.**

Those in favour of capital punishment claim it is a deterrent, stopping at least some people from committing serious crimes. Those against it say it is barbaric and is not a deterrent. Britain, which has no death penalty, has a lower murder rate than the USA.

## FORUM

**People have always disagreed about the rights and wrongs of capital punishment:**

'Executing a murderer is the only way to adequately express our horror at the taking of an innocent life. Nothing else suffices. To equate the lives of killers with those of victims is the worst kind of moral equivalency. If capital punishment is state murder, then imprisonment is state kidnapping and restitution is state theft.'

*Don Feder, author and columnist*

'Does capital punishment tend to the security of the people? By no means. It hardens the hearts of men, and makes the loss of life appear light to them; it renders life insecure, inasmuch as the law holds out that Property is of greater value than life.'

*Elizabeth Fry, Quaker and prison reformer*

*What's your opinion?*

# Chapter 6

# How else can we tackle crime?

There are three distinct areas in which societies work to combat crime: preventing crimes from taking place in the first instance; detecting and solving crimes that do occur; and dealing with convicted criminals. There are new approaches in all of these areas and some of them may have a big impact on fighting crime in the future.

## Investing in the future

Criminology is the study of crime and criminals. It is an academic field that tries to discover why crimes happen and how best to investigate and combat criminal activity. Criminologists look at the causes of all types of crime, and also at the minds and social backgrounds of offenders. The aim is to understand crime, and build this understanding into police work and into crime-prevention methods.

Research has shown that children who are socially disadvantaged and have poor schooling are more likely to grow up to become criminals than those offered better life chances and good schooling. A study in Michigan, USA, found that children who went to a good-quality kindergarten reduced the likelihood that they would commit a violent crime later in life by 50 per cent. This approach involves a long-term view, and investing well in advance to prevent a generation of young people turning to crime, but it is paying off in many countries.

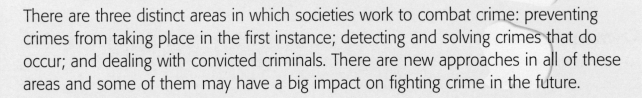

## Expert View

'When kids miss out on early learning, they're more likely to fall behind, drop out and find themselves out of options. That's when they're really at risk to make the wrong decisions and wind up criminals,' Ashenbrenner said. 'With our public safety at stake, we shouldn't gamble with the education of young children. Let's not take any chances and make sure our kids get a great start.'

**Lila Ashenbrenner, Chief of Police,
Hillsboro, Michigan, USA**

The Royal Canadian Mounted Police is one of the most famous police forces in the world and, with their red tunics, also one of the most instantly recognizable. High visibility has distinct advantages when it comes to crime prevention.

## Crime-prevention measures

In the best-possible world, people will not want to turn to crime because they have other, positive, opportunities in life. In reality, though, there will always people who are ready and willing to carry out crimes, no matter how many advantages they have.

Crime prevention involves making it as difficult as possible for people to commit or get away with an offence. Increased security, perhaps in the form of high-visibility policing, aims to deter crime from the outset by increasing the odds of detection. Measures such as CCTV cameras, methods that allow people to report suspicions or give information to the authorities without fear of reprisals, and adding more security checks at airports or train stations and international borders all aim to make criminal activity more difficult and more risky for the perpetrators.

Educational measures can also be effective in reducing the incidence of opportunistic crime – crimes that take place simply because there is an easy opportunity. For example, encouraging householders to keep doors and windows locked reduces the number of thefts from houses; while removing valuable objects, such as radios, satellite-navigation devices and bags, from cars, or at least keeping them out of sight, reduces the number of thefts from unattended vehicles.

## Changing laws

Laws change not only to meet new threats and to acknowledge the passing of old ones, but also to reflect changes in society and social attitudes. Issues that raise moral or ethical considerations often lead to changes in the law. For example, homosexual acts have been legal in Mexico since 1871, but in some parts of the USA only since 2003. In Saudi Arabia homosexual acts carry the death penalty. Each society changes the law (or not) as the predominant beliefs and values of the people change. At present, several countries are in the process of debating and perhaps changing laws relating to taking drugs. There is in many places a change of view that sees drug takers as victims of crime rather than criminals, and in need of medical and social support rather than prosecution and punishment.

## Policing

The racial and ethnic mix of the police force can have an impact on how effective it is in controlling crime levels. For example, having the wealthier and more powerful elements of society and most of the police coming mainly from one racial or ethnic group can lead to tension between the police and other ethnic or racial groups. Police forces in some parts of the world, including the UK, are trying to recruit more officers from ethnic minorities in order to redress the balance and enable people of all backgrounds to identify with and trust the police.

**The figure of Justice is often depicted with a sword and a set of scales. The sword stands for retribution and the scales for balancing arguments around a case.**

## Keeping records

When the police investigate a crime they often gather information about a number of suspects, most of whom are usually found to be innocent of any wrongdoing. This information may take the form of personal details, fingerprints, photographs and, increasingly, DNA samples. The information is stored in a police database where it can be quickly and easily cross-checked. The use of computer systems has greatly aided the fight against crime, but it has also brought with it some problems. People who have not been convicted of a crime may object to their details being held in a police database and may fear that the information could fall into the wrong hands. Careful record keeping and good security procedures are increasingly important aspects of how the police deal with information.

An expert at the FBI's National Laboratory in Boston, USA, examines a DNA record. The printout allows the expert to match this DNA against another sample, perhaps gathered at a crime scene.

## FORUM

**Some experts believe that wielding the stick is the best way to curtail crime, while others believe the carrot is the better approach:**

Should we be tackling the causes by providing:

• Positive opportunities and role models to divert people from crime?

• Good, positive schooling with skilled staff who can relate to offenders, most of whom have poor literacy skills?

• Better support, understanding and resources for offenders?

Or is it better to get tough on crime? As long as offenders are locked away from society, they can do no harm – and that is all that matters. The main thing is to keep society free of criminals and locking them away is the most effective option.

***What's your opinion?***

## Dealing with criminals

There are many ways of dealing with criminals, and different methods are favoured in different countries, each with its own judicial system. Imprisonment remains the most common penalty for all but the most minor crimes. In some countries the prison service is basic and prisoners are given no help with rehabilitation, but in most economically developed countries prison involves at least some element of rehabilitation. A few types of crime are also dealt with by offering offenders the chance to alter their behaviour. One scheme in the UK for dealing with less-serious speeding offences involves offering offenders places on driver re-education programmes as an alternative to the traditional penalties, such as fines. These programmes aim to show the offender why their actions were dangerous and to encourage them not to reoffend in the future.

## Prison reform

Many people – experts and non-experts alike – believe that prison should be reserved only for serious offenders – for those who are a danger to society. This would reduce overcrowding and keep many vulnerable and impressionable young prisoners away from more hardened criminals.

Young, first-time offenders could be confined in residential schools where they could learn the skills needed to improve their employment prospects once they are

**At this detention centre in Nashville, USA, young offenders learn to use computers as part of their rehabilitation. The aim is to give them the skills they need for honest work after their release.**

released. For prison reform to be effective, however, extra resources are needed to tackle the problems of drug-addicted prisoners and those with mental-health issues.

## Restorative justice

One new approach being tried with some criminals is known as restorative justice. This involves bringing offenders and the victims of their crimes face to face. It can be a challenging experience for both parties, but it has proved to be an effective way of showing offenders the impact of their crimes and of reducing the rate of reoffending.

## Ask the offenders

Surveys conducted in many countries over the past ten years have found that a surprising number of ex-offenders feel that the authorities should be tougher on crime. Many feel that a prison sentence alone is not enough to change behaviour. The majority said that the authorities should try to rehabilitate offenders by making them face up to what they have done, suggesting again that restorative justice can make a difference. The act of asking offenders to become involved in crime prevention marks a huge change in society's attitudes towards crime and offenders.

# FORUM

**Some people think prison does not work when it is a 'soft' option, while others think it does not work if it is harsh:**

'For many criminals, prison is . . . actually the soft option that locks them up for a few months in all-expenses-paid accommodation with three meals a day, a gym, pool table and a telly. Then they are free to leave and return to a life of crime – unrepentant, undaunted, undeterred.'

*Simon Hughes, former home affairs spokesman for the UK Liberal Democrat Party*

'The current design of prison systems doesn't work. Overly punitive approaches used on violent, angry criminals only provide a breeding ground for more anger and more violence.'

*Joel Dvoskin, criminal justice expert, University of Arizona, USA*

*What's your opinion?*

# Chapter 7

# What is the future of crime?

While crime has been around since the earliest societies, the types of crime committed and the ways we combat them have changed. Modern technologies and science have opened the door to new criminal opportunities as well as providing new ways to counter them. It is fair to assume that the future holds out the prospect of more new types of criminal activity that we are almost certainly not yet equipped to deal with.

**A competition to hack into a computer system and simulate an attack provides useful information about how to make systems more secure against criminal hackers.**

## Crime and technology

The Internet and modern communications technologies have brought with them new opportunities for many people – including criminals. Criminals are constantly learning how to exploit the Internet in order to commit new crimes – from credit card fraud and identity theft to a range of Internet scams and computer hacking designed to steal data or simply bring down entire computer networks.

As well as making new types of crime possible, the Internet and the mobile phone systems have also made some more traditional crimes easier to commit or more difficult to counter. Offenders can use these new technologies to share and distribute pornography, for example, or to set up drug deals, bully and harass others or plan terrorist activity with a much reduced chance of the authorities becoming aware of their activities in time to do anything about it. Other types of technology are used to clone credit cards, to make fake copies of high-quality objects and to pirate DVDs and CDs.

# FOCUS

### Increase in identity fraud

According to the UK-based fraud-prevention organization Cifas, there was a 40% increase in identity fraud in the first half of 2009. Despite increasingly sophisticated types of online fraud, people still do not safeguard their personal information adequately.

## Cyberterrorism

The Internet also makes the possibility of cyberterrorism more likely. This is the misuse of computers for terrorist purposes. It could involve, for example, taking control of the systems that control the distribution of our water, gas or electricity supplies, telephone services, air-traffic control, rail networks and even nuclear power stations or weapons systems. There has not so far been a successful major assault of this type that we are aware of, but governments around the world are working to keep these vital systems secure.

## Biotechnology and crime

Scientific advances in other areas have been harnessed by the criminals and the authorities alike. As we have already seen, DNA testing can now be used as evidence to prove that someone was at the scene of a crime. But biotechnology can also be exploited by criminals, who, by using trace samples of stolen body tissues, such as a hair left on a chair or a smear of saliva on a glass, can implicate an innocent person in a crime. It's also possible using stolen DNA to run tests to prove, for example, that someone is, or is not, the father of a child, or has a genetic disorder of some sort or is even at a high risk of developing a specific medical condition. This information can then be used for blackmail, for example, or to harm a person's chances of gaining public office or of winning an important promotion at work.

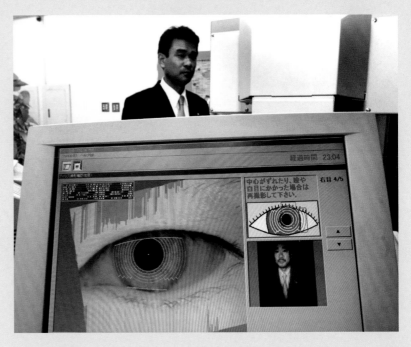

**This is the first ATM machine with iris-recognition technology. It scans and compares the pattern of the user's iris with a stored record of the real cardholder's iris. If the eye scan does not match, the machine will not issue any cash.**

## Sci-fi crime

Nanotechnology and genetic engineering are new sciences, but already it is possible to see how criminals could exploit them. Governments have plans to deal with terrorist attacks that could include the release of an artificially created virus – one that could spread quickly, killing large numbers of people and against which we would have no natural defences. Nanotechnology – working with technology that is so tiny it is manipulated at the molecular level – could also be misused to destroy areas of the environment, or to hold nation states to ransom. As climate change progresses, scarcity of water and food will become increasingly urgent problems in many parts of the world. Already there are disputes over the artificial seeding of clouds to make it rain, as this is seen as 'stealing' the water from other countries or regions.

## Tackling crime in the future

Advances in technology have been adopted by crime-prevention and detection forces around the world. Many urban areas are now covered by closed-circuit television (CCTV) cameras to monitor public activity in the hope of both deterring potential offenders and, if crimes are committed, of recording any evidence. Cameras around the road networks record speeding cars and so aid the fight against dangerous driving, while licence-plate-recognition technology allows CCTV cameras to search automatically for specific vehicles – perhaps those that have been stolen or implicated in a crime.

In an attempt to intercept traffic between criminals on the Internet, many governments use electronic surveillance techniques to monitor at least some email and web use, as well as phone calls and text messaging. Many people feel that

**An array of CCTV cameras observing cars and passers-by. Britain has the highest density of CCTV cameras anywhere in Europe.**

**For women prisoners in Nairobi knitting is part of their rehabilitation, providing a useful, saleable skill that can equip them for life after prison.**

this is a violation of their personal freedom that is not justified by the argument that it is intended to safeguard society. Laws brought in to counter terrorism, similarly, have critics as well as supporters. It is hard to strike the right balance between protecting society and allowing people their individual freedoms.

## What do they know?

DNA profiling is a science in its infancy, but it is likely that in a few years it will be an important tool in the fight against crime. From traces of body fluids or tissues, police may be able to give a basic description of the person they are looking for. It may also be possible to identify people with a tendency to commit some types of crime, and help them from an early age to avoid a life of crime.

Whatever the future holds, the battle against crime will continue, and the scientific work to prevent it will become increasingly important.

### FORUM

**Is increased state surveillance useful or not?**

'Over the past seven years we've been told "nothing to hide, nothing to fear", but a stream of data bungles and abuses of power suggest that even the innocent have a lot to fear.'

*Shami Chakrabarti, Liberty*

'The key is to strike the right balance between privacy, protection and sharing of personal data.'

*UK Home Office*

*What's your opinion?*

# Glossary

**allegation** An untested claim that someone has committed a criminal offence of some type.

**bail** Money that is pledged as a guarantee that a suspect will attend court at an agreed time and place to answer criminal charges.

**banishment** Being sent to live outside one's country, city or social group as a punishment.

**biotechnology** The application of technology to biological systems.

**capital punishment** Being put to death as a penalty for a crime.

**convicted** Found guilty of an offence.

**criminology** The study of crime, criminals and the causes of criminal behaviour.

**curfew** A time after which someone is not allowed outside.

**defence** Argument that a person did not commit the crime of which they are accused.

**detention** Being detained (shut away), usually in prison.

**dictatorship** Political system in which a single person has absolute power, usually because control has been illegally seized.

**DNA** Deoxyribonucleic acid; the chemical that makes up our chromosomes and stores the genetic 'recipe' for an individual.

**DNA profiling** Identifying a person or their likely characteristics from DNA evidence.

**electronic tagging** Fitting an offender with a device that can be tracked electronically so that his or her whereabouts can be monitored.

**ethical** Relating to beliefs about what is right and wrong.

**federal** Relating to the whole nation, rather than states or regions.

**flogging** Punishing with a whip, cord, sticks or other implement.

**forensics** Scientific study of evidence in order to try to solve crime.

**heinous** Very serious.

**Holocaust** The slaughter of Jews, Roma people, homosexuals and some other groups in concentration camps by the German Nazi regime during World War II. The term is now generally used to describe any similar acts.

**honour killing** Murder of someone who is considered to have damaged the honour of a family, by other family members.

**identity theft** Using people's personal details to impersonate them for the purposes of fraud.

**Internet piracy** Using the Internet to acquire illegal copies of copyrighted work, such as books, music or films.

**judicial execution** Killing someone who has been found guilty of a serious offence.

**judicial system** The system a nation employs for imposing laws, trying offenders in a court of law and then administering punishment to those found guilty.

**martyrdom** The act of giving oneself up or suffering a punishment for the benefit of others.

**molecular** Relating to molecules, the small building blocks of matter.

**money laundering** The process of channelling money from criminal activity through a seemingly honest business so that it can enter the economy without arousing suspicion.

**motive** The reason for doing something.

**offender** A person who has committed a crime.

**perpetrate** Carry out a criminal act.

**pornography** Explicit images or writing of a sexual, sometimes violent, nature.

**premeditated** Planned in advance.

**probation officer** A person responsible for monitoring the activity of offenders and people recently released from prison.

**psychology** The scientific study of mental processes.

**rehabilitating** Helping someone to give up criminal behaviour and learn the skills needed to live successfully in society.

**reprisal** An act carried out in revenge.

**restorative justice** System of dealing with offenders that involves bringing them face to face with the victims of their crimes and hearing about the impact of those crimes on the people concerned.

**shanty town** Collection of badly built dwellings that houses poor people, usually found outside a major city.

**sharia** System of laws based on the teachings of the Koran that provides rules for all aspects of life.

**show trial** Unjust trial in which accused people seem to be given the opportunity to have a proper hearing but are in fact unable to defend themselves or affect the outcome.

**statutes** Documents that set out the laws of a country.

**surveillance** Monitoring or watching people, often without their knowledge or permission.

**suspect** Someone who is suspected of having committed a crime but who has not yet been charged or tried.

**tax evasion** Not paying taxes by lying, hiding evidence of income or otherwise cheating the tax system.

**verdict** An innocent or guilty decision at the conclusion of a court case.

**violation** An unjust act that breaches some fair rule or reasonable expectation of behaviour.

# Further information

## Books

*Forensic Science* by Alex Frith, Usborne, 2007

*Teens Take It to Court: Young People Who Challenged the Law – and Changed Your Life* by A Thomas and JD Jacobs, Free Spirit Publishing, 2006

*They Broke the Law – You Be the Judge: True Cases of Teen Crime* by A Thomas and JD Jacobs, Free Spirit Publishing, 2003

*Usborne True Stories: Crime and Detection* by Gill Harvey, Usborne, 2007

*Why do People Commit Crime?* by Alex Woolf, Raintree, 2004

*Women Who Made a Scene: Heroines, Villainesses, Eccentrics* by Lesley James, Raintree, 2000

*Your Government: How it Works: The Federal Bureau of Investigation* by Dynise Balcavage, Chelsea House Publishers, 2000

## Websites

**www.crimereduction.homeoffice.gov.uk/yp/ypgcp06.htm**
A practical guide to crime prevention suitable for the whole family.

**www.crime-scene-investigator.net**
Provides an insight into what a crime-scene investigator actually does.

**www.crimestoppers-uk.org**
An independent charity that is helping to find criminals and solve crimes.

**www.mcgruff-safe-kids.com**
Safety and crime-prevention products for children.

**www.youthjusticenb.ca**
Information on youth justice programs in Canada.

# Index

Entries in **bold** are for pictures.